Getting in Shape
for Cello

by Cassia Harvey

CHP125

©2004 by C. Harvey Publications All Rights Reserved.

www.charveypublications.com - print books
www.learnstrings.com - PDF downloadable books
www.harveystringarrangements.com - chamber music

Less-advanced (A) pages are structured so that they can be played together with more-advanced (B) pages.

Contents

Page			
2	Finger Trainer (A)	30	Exercise for Both Hands (A/B)
3	Little Brown Jug (A)	31	Karobushka (A/B)
4	Finger Trainer (B)	32	Pre-Skipping (A)
5	Little Brown Jug (B)	33	Fireworks Music (A)
6	Finger Workout (A)	34	Pre-Skipping (B)
7	Soldier's Chorus (A)	35	Fireworks Music (B)
8	Finger Workout (B)	36	Skipping (A)
9	Soldier's Chorus (B)	37	Arkansas Traveler (A)
10	Daily Exercise (A)	38	Skipping (B)
11	The Frog Went A-Courting (A)	39	Arkansas Traveler (B)
12	Daily Exercise (B)	40	First Position Workout (A)
13	The Frog Went A-Courting (B)	41	High Cap (A)
14	Finger & Bow Workout (A)	42	First Position Workout (B)
15	Turkish Dance (A)	43	High Cap (B)
16	Finger & Bow Workout (B)	44	Pre-Skipping (A)
17	Turkish Dance (B)	45	Pickles for Breakfast (A)
18	Pre-Skipping (A)	46	Pre-Skipping (B)
19	Hopak (A)	47	Pickles for Breakfast (B)
20	Pre-Skipping (B)	48	Skipping (A)
21	Hopak (B)	49	Chicken on the Fence Post (A)
22	Skipping (A)	50	Skipping (B)
23	Brandenburg 5 (A)	51	Chicken on the Fence Post (B)
24	Skipping (B)	52	First Position Workout (A)
25	Brandenburg 5 (B)	53	Flower Song (A)
26	Strength Exercise (A)	54	First Position Workout (B)
27	Mairi's Wedding (A)	55	Flower Song (B)
28	Strength Exercise (B)	56	Skipping (A)
29	Mairi's Wedding (B)	57	The British Grenadiers (A)
		58	Skipping (B)
		59	The British Grenadiers (B)

Getting in Shape for Cello
Finger Trainer (A)

Cassia Harvey

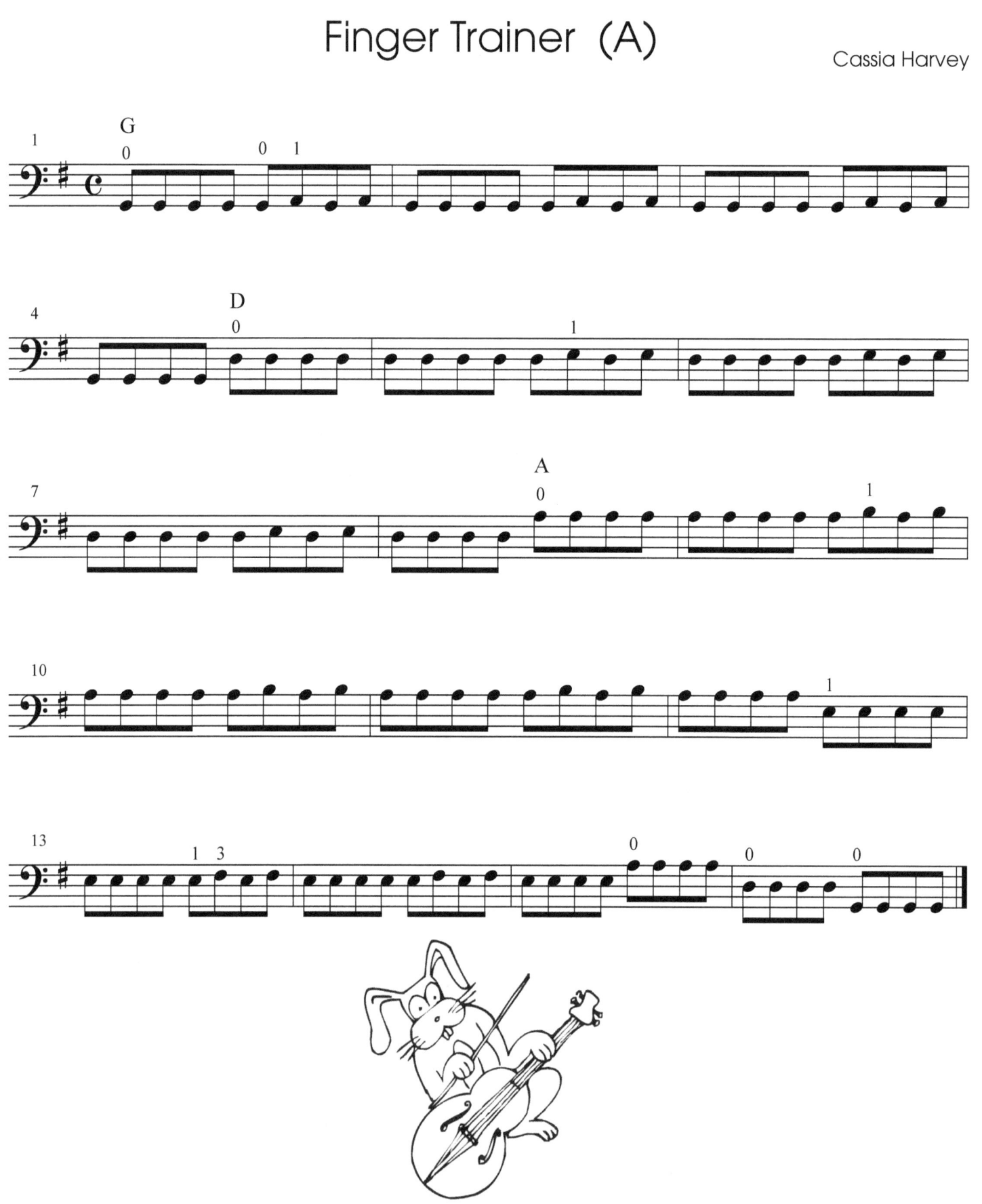

©2004 C. Harvey Publications All Rights Reserved.

Little Brown Jug (A)

Trad./arr. C. Harvey

©2004 C. Harvey Publications All Rights Reserved.

Finger Trainer (B)

Cassia Harvey

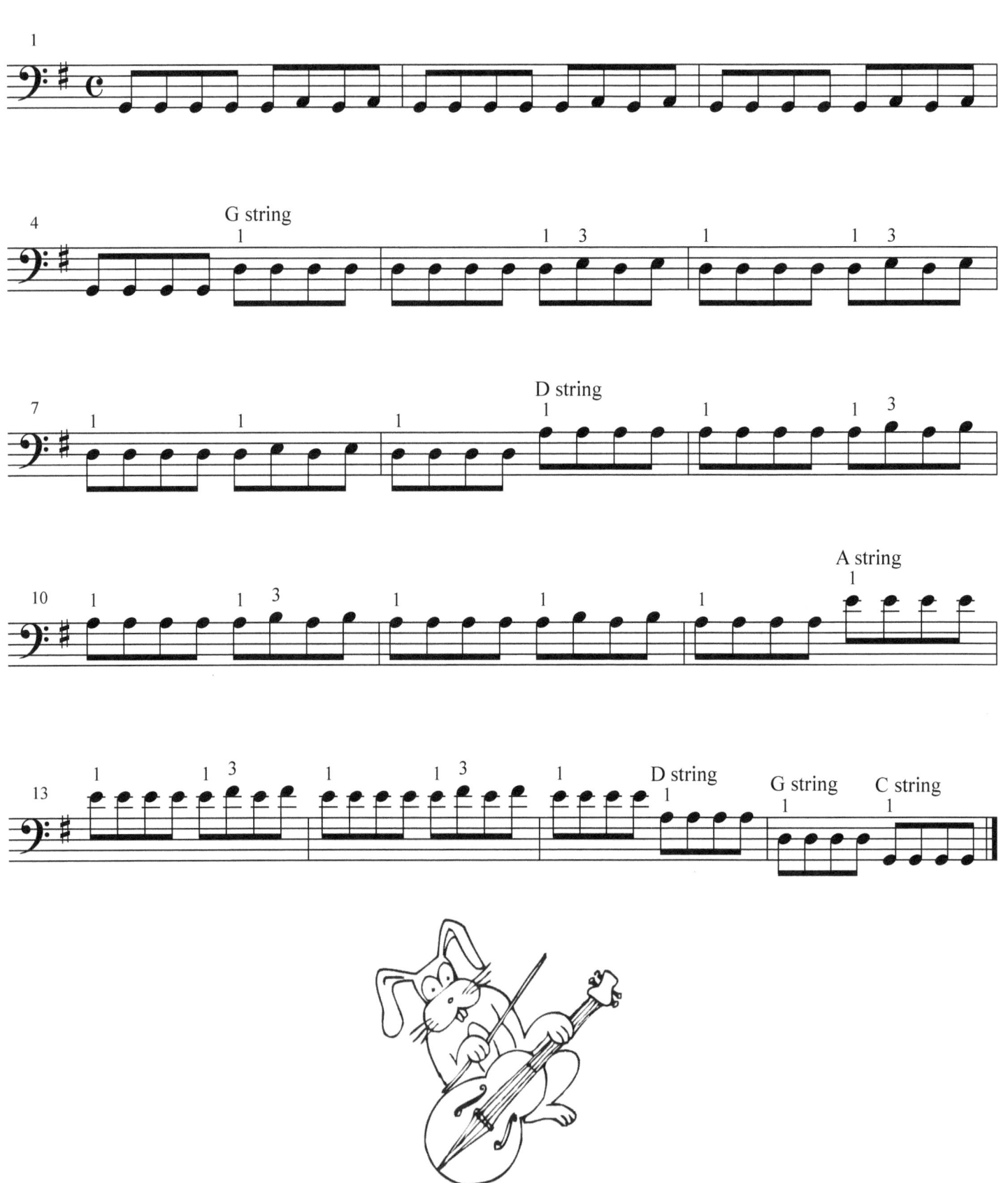

Little Brown Jug (B)

Trad./arr. C. Harvey

©2004 C. Harvey Publications All Rights Reserved.

Finger Workout (A)

Cassia Harvey

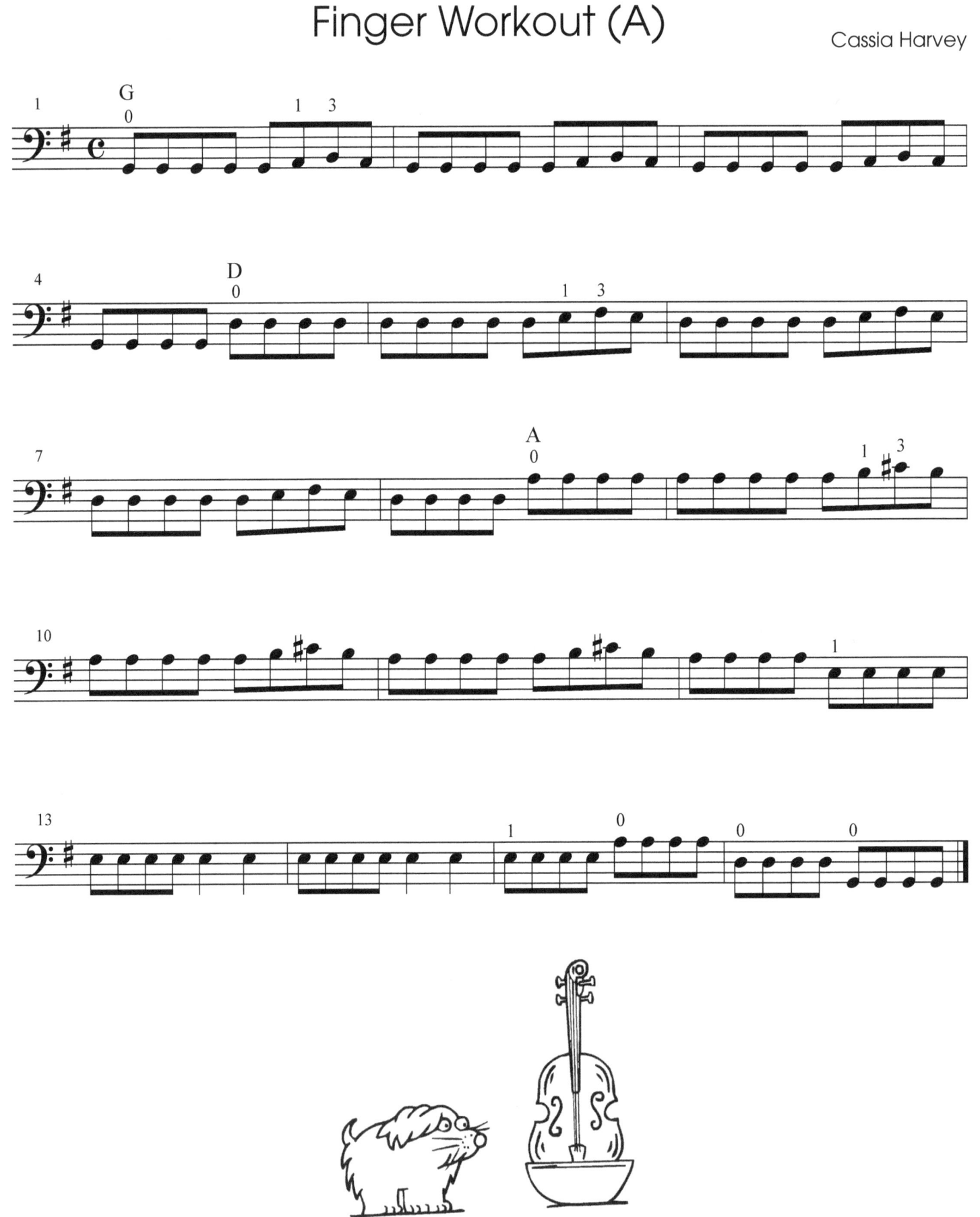

Getting in Shape for Cello

Soldier's Chorus (A)

Bizet/arr. C. Harvey

©2004 C. Harvey Publications All Rights Reserved.

Finger Workout (B)

Cassia Harvey

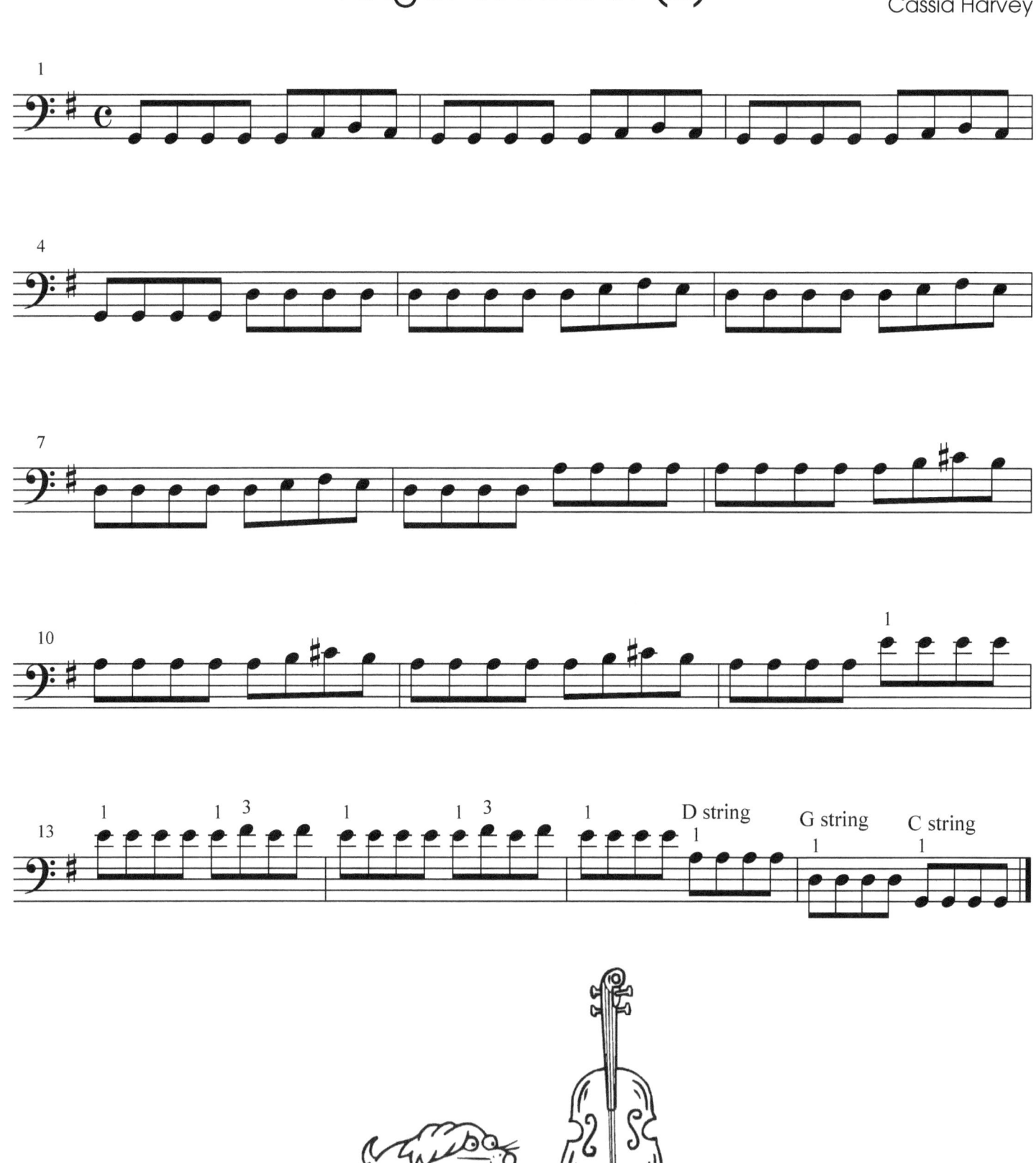

Soldier's Chorus (B)

Bizet/arr. C. Harvey

The Frog Went A-Courting (A)

Trad./arr. C. Harvey

Daily Exercise (B)

Cassia Harvey

The Frog Went A-Courting (B)

Trad./arr. C. Harvey

Finger and Bow Workout (A)

Cassia Harvey

Turkish Dance (A)

Kruckow/arr. C. Harvey

Finger and Bow Workout (B)

Cassia Harvey

Turkish Dance (B)

Kruckow/arr. C. Harvey

Pre-Skipping (A)

Cassia Harvey

Hopak (A)

Mussorgsky/arr. C. Harvey

Pre-Skipping (B)

Cassia Harvey

©2004 C. Harvey Publications All Rights Reserved.

Hopak (B)

Mussorgsky/arr. C. Harvey

Skipping (A)

Cassia Harvey

Brandenburg 5 (A)

Bach/arr. C. Harvey

Brandenburg 5 (B)

Bach/arr. C. Harvey

Mairi's Wedding (A)

Trad./arr. C. Harvey

Strength Exercise (B)

Cassia Harvey

Getting in Shape for Cello

Mairi's Wedding (B)

Trad./arr. C. Harvey

Karobushka (A/B)

Trad./arr. C. Harvey

©2004 C. Harvey Publications All Rights Reserved.

Pre-Skipping (A)

Cassia Harvey

Fireworks Music (A)

Handel/arr. C. Harvey

Pre-Skipping (B)

Cassia Harvey

Getting in Shape for Cello

©2004 C. Harvey Publications All Rights Reserved.

Fireworks Music (B)

Handel/arr. C. Harvey

Skipping (A)

Cassia Harvey

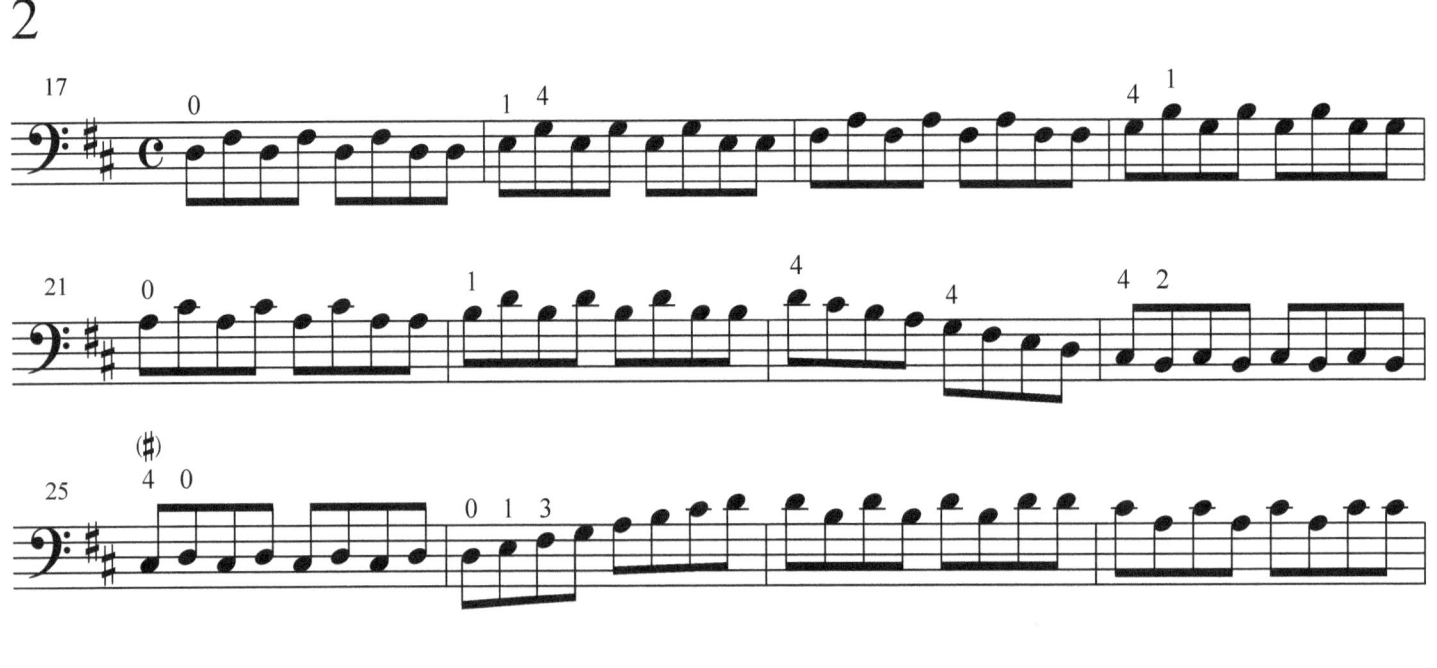

©2004 C. Harvey Publications All Rights Reserved.

Arkansas Traveler (A)

Trad./arr. C. Harvey

©2004 C. Harvey Publications All Rights Reserved.

Skipping (B)

Cassia Harvey

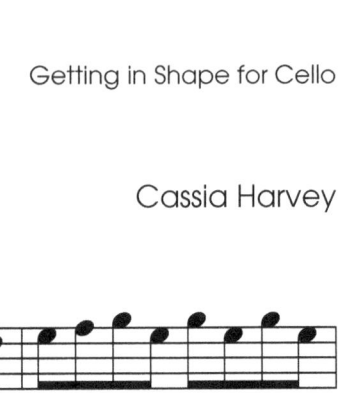

Arkansas Traveler (B)

Trad./arr. C. Harvey

40

Getting in Shape for Cello

First Position Workout (A)

Cassia Harvey

©2004 C. Harvey Publications All Rights Reserved.

High Cap (A)

Trad./arr. C. Harvey

©2004 C. Harvey Publications All Rights Reserved.

First Position Workout (B)

Cassia Harvey

High Cap (B)

Trad./arr. C. Harvey

©2004 C. Harvey Publications All Rights Reserved.

Pre-Skipping (A)

Cassia Harvey

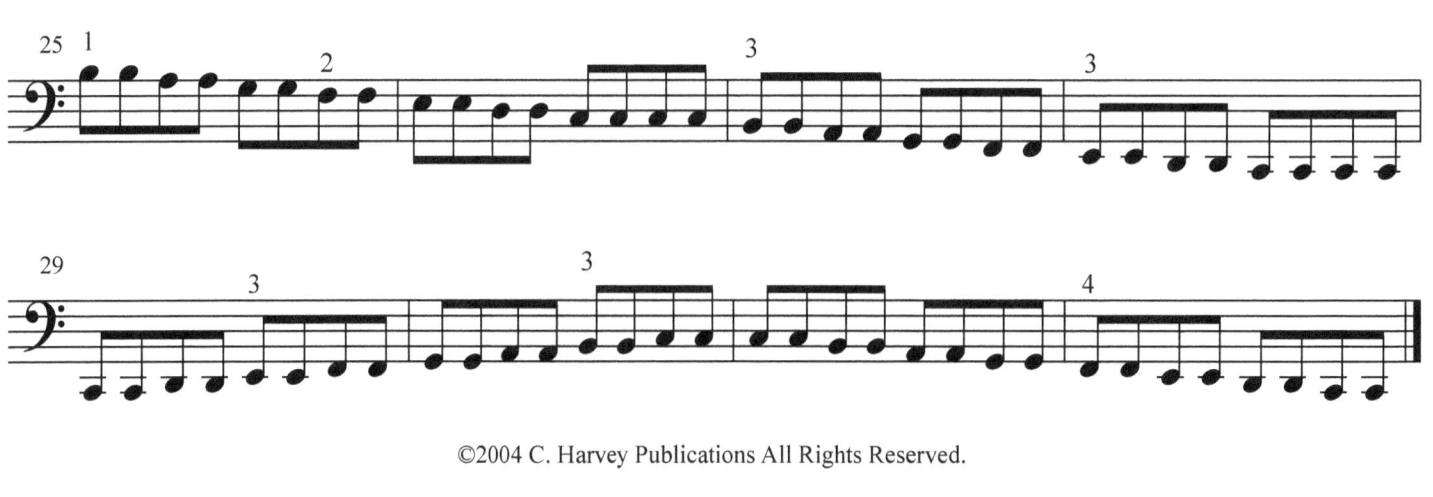

Pickles for Breakfast (A)

Trad./arr. C. Harvey

Pickles for Breakfast (B)

Trad./arr. C. Harvey

Skipping (A)

Cassia Harvey

Chicken on the Fence Post (A)

Trad./arr. C. Harvey

Skipping (B)

Cassia Harvey

Chicken on the Fence Post (B)

Trad./arr. C. Harvey

First Position Workout (A)

Cassia Harvey

©2004 C. Harvey Publications All Rights Reserved.

Flower Song (A)

Trad./arr. C. Harvey

First Position Workout (B)

Cassia Harvey

Flower Song (B)

Trad./arr. C. Harvey

Skipping (A)

Cassia Harvey

The British Grenadiers (A)

Trad./arr. C. Harvey

Skipping (B)

Cassia Harvey

The British Grenadiers (B)

Trad./arr. C. Harvey

Available from www.charveypublications.com
Sailing Into Bethlehem: Compatible Christmas Duets for Strings

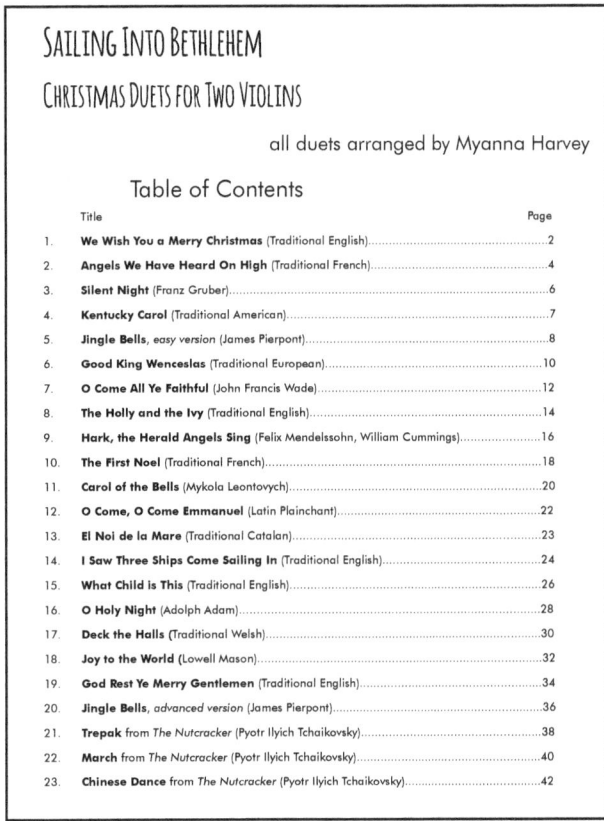

CHP333

CHP334

CHP335